CAMBRIDGE
UNIVERSITY PRESS

Cambridge Lower Secondary

English

WORKBOOK 9

Graham Elsdon

CAMBRIDGE
UNIVERSITY PRESS

University Printing House, Cambridge CB2 8BS, United Kingdom

One Liberty Plaza, 20th Floor, New York, NY 10006, USA

477 Williamstown Road, Port Melbourne, VIC 3207, Australia

314–321, 3rd Floor, Plot 3, Splendor Forum, Jasola District Centre, New Delhi – 110025, India

103 Penang Road, #05-06/07, Visioncrest Commercial, Singapore 238467

Cambridge University Press is part of the University of Cambridge.

It furthers the University's mission by disseminating knowledge in the pursuit of education, learning and research at the highest international levels of excellence.

www.cambridge.org
Information on this title: www.cambridge.org/9781108746694

First published 2014
Second edition 2021

20 19 18 17 16 15 14 13 12 11 10 9 8 7 6

Printed in Italy by Rotolito S.p.A.

A catalogue record for this publication is available from the British Library

ISBN 978-1-108-74669-4 Paperback with Digital Access (1 Year)

Cambridge University Press has no responsibility for the persistence or accuracy of URLs for external or third-party internet websites referred to in this publication, and does not guarantee that any content on such websites is, or will remain, accurate or appropriate. Information regarding prices, travel timetables, and other factual information given in this work is correct at the time of first printing but Cambridge University Press does not guarantee the accuracy of such information thereafter.

....

> Contents

> How to use this book

This workbook provides questions for you to practise what you have learnt in the Learner's Book. There is a unit to match each unit in your Learner's Book. Each session is divided into three parts:

Focus: these questions help you to master the basics ———————▶

Practice: these questions help you to become more confident in using what you have learnt ———————▶

Challenge: these questions will make you think hard ———————▶

Focus

1   Note down any connotations or associations with the word 'river'.

....

....

....

2   Read the extract on the next page from a novel called *The Current*. A river is used as a motif throughout the story. Summarise how the river is used to represent aspects of the narrator's life.

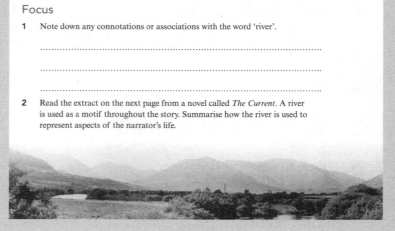

Practice

3   Now read another extract, this time from the middle of the novel. Analyse how the motif has been developed.

> Sometimes, things happen all at once. Francesca had started to feel unwell earlier that week, and within days they were operating on her. James was away at university by this time and I was on my own. As I walked through the fields that night, I didn't know what would happen. The wind raged and the river was swollen with rainwater. The water rose, threatening to burst the banks. Torrents of water tossing around sharp branches raged downstream.

....

....

....

Challenge

4   Write another short section of the story *The Current* that includes the motif of the river to show ideas and themes. You could describe Francesca leaving the hospital or a marriage that takes place. Write 80–100 words.

....

....

....

....

....

....

....

1 ▶ Going underground

〉 1.1 Relic

Writers deliberately choose what information to reveal to the reader about certain characters. For example, they might give explicit information about a character's circumstances so the reader can work out why that character takes certain actions later on.

Focus

1 Read this extract from *Darkparis*. Underline the key information about Louis's apartment, then briefly summarise the impression this extract creates of Louis's life.

> Louis opened the door to his apartment and switched on the light. Everything was organised and neat. Everything was in its place. The walls were painted cream and the little kitchen was perfectly clean. Most people would think it a very pleasant apartment. But for the first time, Louis noticed how bare it looked. Table, chairs, TV, rug, clock . . . it seemed somehow empty. He stood for a moment and listened to the silence. He had lived here for almost a year. The only photograph in the room was of a smiling Louis with his school friends. They'd gradually lost contact over the months. In that moment he decided – he would go to meet Relic.

....

....

....

....

....

....

Practice

2   Reread the final sentence of the extract, then write a paragraph explaining why you think Louis decides to meet Relic. Comment on how the information in the rest of the extract helps you understand his decision. Use quotations in your answer.

....

....

....

....

....

....

....

Challenge

3   In your notebook, write a paragraph like the one from *Darkparis*, in which you provide details about a character's actions or surroundings to allow the reader to work things out about them. You could use this image to inspire you, or come up with an idea of your own.

› 1.2 The Doorkeeper

Language focus

Punctuation can be used for rhetorical purposes. This means that punctuation marks such as question marks, exclamation marks and ellipses can shape an argument or suggest something about a character or situation.

A question mark can be used to signal a rhetorical question. It can also create a variety of tones, such as making a speaker sound slightly threatening or surprised ('Why on earth did you make that choice?').

Exclamation marks can also create different effects, such as excitement ('Welcome to your new life!') or anger ('I insist you leave now!').

Ellipses may suggest a variety of emotions or moods, such as nervousness/ hesitation ('Please . . . can I leave now?') or a sense of drama ('And now . . . here it is!').

Focus

1   Read the following conversation between the characters Louis and Relic from *Darkparis*. Explain how ellipses, question marks and exclamation marks help to suggest things about the characters' attitudes and feelings.

> 'Relic,' whispered Louis. 'I'm . . . I'm not sure about this . . . Where are we going?'
>
> 'Haven't I already explained?' said Relic.
>
> They walked in silence. Then Louis asked how much further it was.
>
> 'You don't have to be here, you know. In fact, go home!' Relic declared sharply.

....

....

....

....

....

....

Practice

2   Rewrite the following extract, altering the punctuation and adding ellipses and exclamation marks to help suggest the characters' personalities.

> 'Stand back and watch carefully,' said The Doorkeeper in hushed tones. 'You've waited your whole life for this.'
>
> Louis held his breath and watched as The Doorkeeper slowly turned a key in a door in the wall and pushed it open. Louis stared in horror at the awful thing that appeared.
>
> 'What is that?' whispered Louis, barely breathing.

....

....

....

....

....

....

....

....

Challenge

3 Write a paragraph that follows on from the extract in Activity 2. You can decide what happens. Use dialogue that includes ellipses, question marks and exclamation marks to suggest the characters' attitudes and feelings.

....

....

....

....

....

....

....

....

....

....

› 1.3 Reviewing *Darkparis*

When analysing two or more texts together, you need first to locate information, then summarise it. The next stage is to synthesise it, which means bringing details together to find links and make overall points.

Focus

1 Here are two reviews of *Darkparis*. Using two different colours, highlight the positive and negative points made in each review.

> **Floyd:** The ending of this book is amazing. It was the character of The Doorkeeper that grabbed my interest at first, because he seemed so mysterious, and that's what kept me reading because I wanted to find out who he was and why he needed Louis to help him. I did lose a bit of interest in the middle of the book — the bit where The Doorkeeper goes missing — but in the last few chapters, there are so many things happening and when The Doorkeeper came back and said his last words, it was brilliant.

> **Hyen:** Like my friends, I mostly enjoyed *Darkparis*. The ending of the book wasn't as good as I'd hoped, but the character of The Doorkeeper was the best in the story. I liked the way he was mysterious, but also was weak too and needed the help of other people to survive. The middle chapters of the book, where the setting changes to the island, were my favourite part. Relic was interesting too — I think the writer should have involved her more in the story.

Practice

2 Briefly summarise the positive and negative points from the two reviews in the Focus activity in one paragraph.

....

....

....

....

....

....

Challenge

3   The publishers of *Darkparis* have said this about the book: 'Everyone who reads the book thinks it's the best thing they've read.'

Using the information from the previous activities, explain whether you think this is true and why. Use examples from the reviews in Activity 1 in your answer.

....

....

....

....

....

....

....

....

....

....

> 1.4 The second test

One key choice made by a playwright is how much information to give to the audience at various points in the play. Withholding information can be an important device for creating effects such as mystery or tension.

Focus

1   Read the following scene from a script. You should then complete the two tables to identify what information Louis and the audience do or do not have.

> LOUIS *is in a large underground area. He is walking slowly along a pathway. His hands are tied behind his back and he has a blindfold covering his eyes.*
>
> LOUIS   Hello? Is anyone there?
>
> *Around the next corner,* THE DOORKEEPER *and* RELIC *can hear* LOUIS *approaching.*
>
> THE DOORKEEPER   (*to* RELIC) This will be a real test for him. Then we'll know.
>
> LOUIS *turns the corner. Further down the path, there is a gap that leads a long way down under the earth.* LOUIS *continues walking slowly towards it.*

What Louis knows	What Louis does not know

What the audience knows	What the audience does not know

Practice

2 What effects are created by the different levels of knowledge that the character and the audience have? Write a summary, explaining:

- how you feel towards Louis

- how you feel towards The Doorkeeper and Relic

- what you still do not know by the end of the scene.

....

....

....

....

....

....

Challenge

3   Write your own brief scene like the one in the Focus activity, in which the characters and the audience have different levels of knowledge. Structure your scene to create different effects. You could use this idea or one of your own:

A boy is proudly walking down a street in his best clothes. His mischievous younger brothers are hiding in a bush with a hosepipe . . .

....

....

....

....

....

....

....

....

....

....

> 1.5 Visiting Coober Pedy

Language focus

Writers often make comparisons to help readers picture or understand a topic. Literary techniques such as simile and metaphor are particularly effective ways of making comparisons, and writers may repeat and develop a comparison throughout a text as an extended metaphor. Look at this example from a piece of travel writing. The writer uses water-based comparisons to show the heat of a desert town:

- The haze of heat distorted Mandora, making the town look like it was under water. In the dazzling light, the shape of human bodies seemed to shift as waves of heat rippled. People swam slowly towards me, their limbs flailing and their faces made wide by the watery midday world.

Notice how the references to water and swimming contribute to the overall purpose of the description. The comparison shows the reader clearly how hot it is in the desert, as well as how the power of nature can alter the way we perceive our surroundings.

Focus

1   Read the following paragraph from a piece of travel writing, then briefly explain what the city of Dhaka is being compared to. Tentacles are long arms.

The tentacles of Dhaka

The glowing red eyes of the two towers in the distance stared at me. Above them, a huge head of smoke hung. This city was dangerous. I had to escape, but everywhere I turned, the tentacles of Dhaka reached out for me. The streets pounded like a heartbeat below my feet, and the threatening growl of the city was everywhere. Dhaka had me in its sights. I was its prey.

....

....

Practice

2 Explain the effect and overall impact of the extended metaphor in the passage. What impression does it create of the city and of the narrator's state of mind?

....

....

....

....

....

....

....

....

Challenge

3   Write a description of a place using an extended metaphor. You could base
    your writing on the picture on the previous page or use an idea of your own.

....

....

....

....

....

....

> 1.6 Living under the ground

Towards the end of a piece of travel writing, the writer usually sums up what their
travels have taught them about the places they visited, as well as commenting on
human life and culture.

Focus

1   Read the last paragraph of a learner's piece of travel writing about Matmata.
    Tick the statement(s) on the next page that best describe what it shows.

Leaving Matmata

Climbing back in to the sunshine, I felt I'd changed. Having spent a week underground,
I found out that these local people, who I thought were going to be very different to
me, were very much the same in lots of ways. They wanted their families to be happy,
and they wanted to be healthy. I looked back at the person I was before I came here,
and felt slightly ashamed. As I drove away back to my beautiful home and nice life,
the villagers waved me off with smiles and good wishes.

a There are many different ways of living, and they are all equal. ☐

b In the modern world, it is difficult to live without modern facilities. ☐

c People who live privileged lives are often patronising. ☐

d Humans have the same feelings and ambitions wherever they live. ☐

e Modern living is destroying old ways of living. ☐

Practice

2 Write a paragraph explaining why you chose the statement(s) you did in the Focus activity. Use details from the text in your explanation.

....

....

....

....

....

....

Challenge

3 Now write the important final paragraph of a piece of travel writing yourself, based on this description. Experiment with different ways of ordering the paragraph to achieve the effect you want.

Imagine you are leaving the busy city of Shanghai by train and are reflecting on the week you spent there. At first you found it difficult being in such a busy place, but you have met many friendly, helpful people in Shanghai.

....

....

....

....

....

....

....

....

....

2 ▶ Law and order

⟩ 2.1 Right and wrong

Remember that there are four main sentence types: simple, compound, complex and compound-complex. Writers choose and position different sentence types carefully to support their purpose. Look at the example below, where a compound sentence is followed by a complex sentence:

- Humans rely on others and they benefit from cooperation. Although humans can sometimes be selfish, working together is essential for human survival.

The first sentence provides key facts for the reader to focus on, then the second sentence develops and extends the point, providing an explanation. Together, they help the reader understand the point and convey the information in a gradual way.

Now look at this example, in which a compound-complex sentence is followed by a simple sentence:

- Although humans can sometimes be selfish, working together is important for human survival and also for social well-being. Cooperation between humans is essential.

Here, the detail is given in the first sentence and the second sentence reinforces the main point. The effect of this is to sum up and direct the reader to the overall message in the text.

Focus

1 Explain the effect of the following combinations of sentence types.

a A conscience encourages good behaviour. Although humans have their own selfish needs, we are also aware of the needs of others, and a conscience helps us decide how to accommodate both.

....

....

....

....

b I thought carefully about what I wanted to do and then thought about how it might hurt my friend, and although it was a difficult decision, I knew what I had to do. My friendship was more important.

....

....

....

....

Practice

2   Here is a short paragraph written in simple sentences. Rewrite the paragraph using a combination of different sentence types to make the text more engaging.

> Emotions are powerful things. Emotions can be positive feelings. Emotions can be negative feelings. Emotions can influence people's decisions. People's consciences are influenced by emotions.

....

....

....

....

....

....

....

Challenge

3   Write an imaginative account about a time when you had to make a difficult decision. Use a combination of sentence types. You could use example b from Activity 1 as a model for varying your sentences.

....

....

....

....

....

··

··

··

··

··

❯ 2.2 Join the police

Language focus

Colons and semi-colons are mainly used to help organise information in sentences. However, these punctuation marks can also be used for deliberate effect. For example, consider the difference between these two sentences:

- Police officers are very aware of one key thing about applying the law and that is fairness.

- Police officers are very aware of one key thing about applying the law: fairness.

Both sentences are correctly punctuated, but the colon in the second sentence strongly emphasises the word 'fairness' by making the reader pause before saying it.

Semi-colons can also suggest a relationship between ideas and give different shades of meaning. For example:

- Police officers are there to serve their community. Looking after people is the key part of their job.

- Police officers are there to serve their community; looking after people is the key part of their job.

The full stop in the middle of the first example gives the statement a factual tone. It invites the reader to stop, creating a 'distance' between the two ideas. In the second example, the semi-colon functions like the word 'because'. It brings the ideas closer together and emphasises the link between service, community and caring for others.

Focus

1 Insert the missing colon in the following sentences to emphasise the key words.

    a The community expects one thing from police officers fairness.

    b Dedication and bravery the two main attributes of any good police officer.

2 Rewrite the following sentences, inserting a semi-colon to suggest a link between the two parts of the sentence. Remove words if necessary to create grammatically correct sentences.

    a Communities need good police officers because good police officers make good communities.

       ....

       ....

    b Communities are complex things and they need time and care invested in them.

       ....

       ....

       ....

       ....

Practice

3   Explain the effect of the colons and semi-colon in the following sentences.

   a   This is what I am certain of: job satisfaction is the most important aspect of any career.

   ....

   ....

   b   Policing: interesting, complicated and rewarding. Some of the time it can be frustrating; most of the time it is the best job in the world.

   ....

   ....

   ....

   ....

Challenge

4   Write a paragraph about your dream career. Use colons and semi-colons for effect in your writing.

   ....

   ....

   ....

   ....

   ....

   ....

   ....

   ....

> 2.3 The art detective

Good descriptive writing often appeals to a reader's five senses to bring a setting or event to life. It also focuses on creating an effective mood or atmosphere to capture and keep the reader's attention.

Focus

1   In the space below, create a spider diagram or mind map of things you can sense in the room you are sitting in. What can you see, hear, smell and touch?

2   Add to your diagram to include the emotions you are experiencing – are you excited, tired, stressed? What can you feel – is the room hot or cold, for example?

Practice

3   Using your notes, write a paragraph describing your situation at this moment. Start by establishing a feeling or atmosphere. Choose language carefully to capture this mood.

....

....

....

....

....

....

....

....

Challenge

4   Now practise your descriptive skills by writing about an unfamiliar situation.

In your notebook, write a descriptive paragraph of about 100 words based on this picture. Remember to focus on creating an atmosphere.

> 2.4 Young detectives

The personality of the main character or characters is a key part of detective fiction. The type of person a detective is affects how they go about solving the mystery.

Focus

1   Read the following extract from the opening of a detective story called *Broken Promises*. Write a summary of what it reveals about the personality of the detective, Lian.

> Lian quietly knocked on the door, and waited. She knew the owner of the shop, Mr Chan, a large, unfriendly man who was always getting into arguments with people. But now he was in need of help. Jewellery – and lots of it – had been stolen from his shop the previous evening.
>
> Mr Chan opened the door. 'Wondered when you'd bother to turn up,' he said abruptly.
>
> Lian said nothing but entered the shop, stepping quietly behind Mr Chan. He walked like an angry bear. She let him talk.
>
> 'They got in through this window. I called you lot twelve times. Where have you been?' he demanded.
>
> Lian said nothing, but looked carefully at the broken window and the way the glass lay on the floor. She knew straight away.
>
> 'I think I can solve this very quickly,' she said quietly, as she confidently looked Mr Chan right in the eye. Mr Chan blinked and for once, said nothing.

....

....

....

....

....

....

Practice

2   Fictional characters usually develop throughout a story. In the extract in
Activity 1, the balance of power between Lian and Mr Chan changes between
the start and the final sentence.

Using quotations to support your ideas, explain how Lian develops and what
the text implies about her.

....

....

....

....

....

....

Challenge

3   In your notebook, write your own scene from the opening of a detective story.
In it, you should show the personalities of the characters and some details
about the mystery that needs to be solved. You should write at least 12 lines.
You could use the following idea or one of your own:

**Kwame is a confident, easy-going policeman. He arrives at an old lady's
house. Her handbag has gone missing and she is very upset.**

> 2.5 Making deductions

A character study is a piece of analysis that gives information and comments on a character in a story. Character studies include information about how characters develop and the typical ways readers respond to the character.

Focus

1   Read the extract from *Broken Promises* again. As you read, make notes around the text on Mr Chan's background, his appearance and the way he speaks.

> Lian quietly knocked on the door, and waited. She knew the owner of the shop, Mr Chan, a large, unfriendly man who was always getting into arguments with people. But now he was in need of help. Jewellery – and lots of it – had been stolen from his shop the previous evening.
>
> Mr Chan opened the door. 'Wondered when you'd bother to turn up,' he said abruptly.
>
> Lian said nothing but entered the shop, stepping quietly behind Mr Chan. He walked like an angry bear. She let him talk.
>
> 'They got in through this window. I called you lot twelve times. Where have you been?' he demanded.
>
> Lian said nothing, but looked carefully at the broken window and the way the glass lay on the floor. She knew straight away.
>
> 'I think I can solve this very quickly,' she said quietly, as she confidently looked Mr Chan right in the eye. Mr Chan blinked and for once, said nothing.

Practice

2 Make some notes about the different ways in which readers might respond to Mr Chan. What might they assume about him based on how the writer has presented him in the extract?

....

....

....

....

Challenge

3 Effective character studies begin with an overview of the character's role in the story before providing details. By the end of *Broken Promises*, Mr Chan is confirmed to be the villain – he has faked the theft of his own jewellery.

Based on the extract in Session 2.4, write a character study of Mr Chan in your notebook. You should write at least 12 lines. You could begin:

In the story, Mr Chan seems to be a victim, but actually turns out to be the villain. From the opening of the story, readers view him with suspicion.

› 2.6 Detective fiction

Biased texts deliberately present a partial or unfair opinion. Writers of biased texts avoid presenting views or facts that contradict their own. When considering bias, it is important to think about who has written a text and why they have written it.

Focus

1   Place a tick to show which of these writers are likely to produce a biased text.

> Jacob is writing a book about people's attitudes towards detective stories. Jacob is a writer of detective stories and has said in interviews that he thinks most people love to read this type of stories above all others. His book will also contain views from his friends who are also writers. ☐

> Anika is studying English at university. She is researching people's attitudes towards detective fiction. She has read lots of studies from other researchers and has interviewed people with a range of opinions. The book will contain statistics and analysis to show different views on the topic. ☐

> Boris has been asked to write an article for a magazine about the public's attitudes to detective fiction. The man who owns the magazine (and who will be paying Boris for the article) owns a big book company that publishes lots of detective fiction. ☐

Practice

2 Read the online review of the new detective fiction book *Broken Promises* by Mae Liu. The review has been written by another writer whose books are published by a different company.

Use three colours to highlight words and phrases that seem:

- factual

- fair opinions

- biased views.

This story is another in the series featuring Lian Yang, the quiet but effective detective. Most fans of the genre know the character of Lian, as the book sales of 500 000 for Liu's previous novel suggest. *Broken Promises* is not the best of books, however. From the start, where Yang investigates a break-in at the shop of the suspicious Mr Chan, it feels very predictable. Familiar openings are, of course, common in detective stories, but this opening – and indeed the whole book – is poor and confirms that Mae Liu is past her best. Anyone who reads this will be sorely disappointed. There are so many better writers producing much better detective fiction.

Challenge

3 Would you describe the review in Activity 2 as biased? Explain your thoughts, using quotations from the text.

....

....

....

....

....

....

....

....

....

....

....

....

....

....

3 'The Red-Headed League'

> 3.1 The red-headed visitor

Language focus

In older texts, you may come across unfamiliar words. There are several ways in which you can try and work out their meaning.

Context is a good starting point – read the words around the unfamiliar word in the sentence and also think about what is happening in the story at that point. For example, consider the sentence, *There was nothing remarkable about the man save his blazing red head*. You know that the speaker is making a comment on someone's appearance, so you can make a sensible guess that 'remarkable' means 'distinctive' or 'noticeable'.

You can also use your knowledge of morphology. In the case of 'remarkable', you can see that the pattern of the word suggests that is made up of three parts – the prefix 're-', the root word 'mark' and the suffix '-able'. Using word patterns and etymology, you may work out that 're-' means 'again', 'marquer' is French for 'note', and '-able' means 'capable of'.

Finally, thinking about similar words can help you work out the meaning of a word you don't know. For example, you might be familiar with the words 'remark', 'marked' or 'marking', which will give you a clue that 'remarkable' is connected to ideas of 'comment on' and 'noticeable'.

Focus

1   Research the etymology and meaning of the following words and complete the table.

Word	Meaning	Etymology
analysis		
liberty		
destroy		
psyche		
edifice		

Practice

2   Combining your knowledge of morphology and word families, along with your skills of reading in context, write a definition of the underlined words in the this text.

> Sherlock Holmes, the pre-eminent fictional detective of his generation is renowned for his <u>analytical</u> abilities. The stories are written and set in London, and references to that city are used <u>liberally</u> throughout the texts. Holmes's main aim is to curb the <u>destructive</u> criminal habits of his enemies, of which the most famous is the villain Moriarty. Their confrontations are often <u>psychological</u> in nature, with each man trying to outsmart the other. Holmes's desire to defeat criminals is as much about his own <u>edification</u> as it is about keeping society safe.

a   analytical: ....

b   liberally: ....

c   destructive: ....

d   psychological: ....

e   edification: ....

Challenge

3   Now extend your skills by working out and writing definitions for the following words that appear in the text in Activity 2.

a   pre-eminent: ....

b   renowned: ....

c   curb: ....

d   confrontations: ....

e   outsmart: ....

> 3.2 The assistant

Writers use characters in stories for a range of reasons. In mystery stories, a character is often introduced to build the sense of mystery or suspicion.

Focus

1   Using your own words, explain what this sentence means:

Mysterious characters are effective in helping to entertain the reader: when a mysterious character is introduced, the reader anticipates danger or expects problems to occur.

....

....

....

Practice

2   Read the following extract from *Purple Night*, a mystery story by Mae Liu. The story is about Mr Crick, a character with a secret. At this point in the structure of the narrative, Mrs Crick is introduced.

Explain how Mrs Crick is made to seem mysterious and what effect this has on you as a reader.

Mr Crick woke up early and left the house as quietly as he could. He thought that Mrs Crick, his long-suffering, dark-haired wife was still asleep. But she wasn't. To her husband, Mrs Crick was a quiet woman who never asked too many questions, but as she lay there in bed listening to the door close, she took a deep breath and knew what she had to do. This moment had been coming for some time. She got up and peered through the gap in the curtains and watched her husband walk down the street and get into a waiting car. Mrs Crick smiled thinly, and dialled the number – the one she hoped she would never have to dial – and waited for someone to answer. When a voice answered, she uttered the code word, rang off . . . and shed a silent tear.

....

....

....

....

....

....

....

....

Challenge

3   Write your own paragraph describing a mysterious
     character. Try to make the reader feel suspicious of
     them. You could base your paragraph on the man in
     the picture, or use an idea of your own.

....

....

....

....

....

....

....

....

....

....

....

....

....

....

....

....

> 3.3 The end of the League

Reports are formal documents that aim to give clear, logical and direct information.
They are structured and written to help the reader understand the information as
easily as possible.

Focus

1   List five common structural and language features you might find in a report.

....

....

....

....

....

2 Explain how these features help the reader.

....

....

....

....

....

Practice

3 Here is a list of information about the fictional character Sherlock Holmes, created by Sir Arthur Conan Doyle. Read the list, then plan how you could organise this information into a clear, structured report that explains who Sherlock Holmes is and why the stories might be so popular. You can annotate the text and use the write-on lines on the next page to make a plan.

- The first story featuring Holmes was called 'A Study in Scarlet' and was published in 1887.

- Conan Doyle based the character of Holmes on Joseph Bell, his old university professor.

- Holmes lives at 221B Baker Street with his housekeeper, Mrs Hudson, and he plays the violin.

- There are 56 short stories and four novels that feature Holmes.

- Holmes has a brother, Mycroft, who is even more intelligent than Sherlock.

- Holmes's arch-enemy is Professor Moriarty; in a story called 'The Final Problem', they confront each other in Switzerland.

- When Conan Doyle stopped writing Holmes stories in 1893, fans were very upset and he was persuaded to write some more.

- There have been many stage, TV and film versions of the Sherlock Holmes stories – he is the most portrayed character in film history.

- More than 60 million copies of the books have been sold.

....

....

....

....

....

....

....

....

....

....

....

....

....

....

Challenge

4 Now write your report in your notebook. Remember to use typical language and structural features. You can use additional information from other sources if you wish. You should write at least 12 lines.

> 3.4 Investigating the street

Mystery stories often build to a climax – tension builds as one or more of the characters faces danger. This is followed by a sense of release as the danger ends.

Focus

1   Write definitions for each of these terms:

  a   tension: ....

  b   climax: ....

  c   release: ....

2   Explain how readers are likely to react to the use of tension, climax and release in a story.

....

....

....

....

....

....

....

....

Practice

3   Read another extract from *Purple Night*. In it, the story reaches a climax. Lian, an investigator who has discovered Mr Crick's dangerous secret, arrives to confront him. Use three different colours to highlight the phases of tension, climax and release.

Lian put her foot on the bottom step as quietly as she could. He must be upstairs. The stair creaked a little. Should she be doing this? She was on her own and Crick was dangerous. She'd asked for help, but her nearest colleagues were on another job in another part of town. The second stair creaked. What was that? It sounded like movement upstairs. Lian began to crawl up the stairs on her hands and knees. Maybe she was wrong. Maybe Crick was long gone. One more step. Then it happened. There was an almighty roar as Crick raced towards her. She moved quickly, but he had her cornered. She stood no chance. He was nearly twice her size. So this is it, thought Lian. He smiled menacingly and walked towards her.

'Stop right there, Mr Crick!' demanded a voice from the bottom of the stairs. They had arrived just in time.

4   Analyse the balance between the tension, climax and release parts of the story. Which is the longest phase and what is the effect of this on the reader?

....

....

....

....

....

....

Challenge

5   Using the passage in Activity 3 as a model, write your own paragraph featuring sections of tension, climax and release. You could write about a car chase or use an idea of your own.

....

....

....

....

....

....

....

....

....

....

....

> 3.5 The dark cellar

Language focus

As well as visual images, aural and tactile images can help establish a distinctive atmosphere and help readers to imagine a scene. For example, when writing about scary situations, using aural imagery to refer to quiet, mysterious sounds can establish and build tension:

- Somewhere in the distance, I could hear the sound of a small animal moving slowly, its claws scraping across the stone floor.

The slow speed of the animal and uncertainty about what it is helps to create a fearful sensation.

Now read this example of tactile imagery:

- In the dark, I could feel the spider scuttle rapidly across my hand.

Here, the fear of spiders that many people naturally have is increased by the reference to movement and speed. Notice that in both examples, the lack of visual description of the animal and the spider heightens the sense of fear.

Focus

1   Use two different colours to highlight the aural and tactile images in
the following description, then summarise what they suggest about the
surroundings and the weather.

> ### The long walk
>
> Way up ahead, I could just see the lights of the old house. It seemed miles away, and it
> was dark. I walked across the field, the creaking of the branches filling the air, and behind
> them, the rustle of the leaves. It was a terrible night. The spikes of rain were hitting my
> face and running off down the back of my neck, making me shiver. The house didn't seem
> to be getting closer. As the field got wetter, my boots squelched in the mud. And then,
> somewhere up ahead, a wild animal howled . . .

....

....

....

....

....

....

....

Practice

2   Now summarise the overall effect of these images. What impact do they have
on you and what is being suggested about the character's feelings?

....

....

....

....

....

....

....

....

....

Challenge

3 In your notebook, write your own piece of description containing aural and tactile images. You could use this picture to inspire you or use an idea of your own.

> 3.6 The solution

At the end of mystery stories, the moral emerges. This means that the reader sees what point the writer is making about the way that humans behave. What happens at the end of the story reinforces ideas about moral themes such as good and evil.

Focus

1 Here is a summary of what might happen at the end of *Purple Night*. What moral message do you think the story is giving about crime and punishment?

- Lian, the investigator, has worked out Mr Crick's dangerous secret and tracks him down to a house.

- She arrives at the house and Mr Crick confronts her, but police arrive just in time.

- Mr Crick is arrested, but escapes and drives away in a stolen police car.

- Mr Crick drives off but is caught when the car breaks down.

3 'The Red-Headed League'

....

....

....

....

....

....

Practice

2 Here is different ending to *Purple Night*.

•   Lian, the investigator, has worked out Mr Crick's dangerous secret and tracks him down to a house.

•   She arrives at the house and Mr Crick confronts her, but police arrive just in time.

•   Mr Crick is arrested and put on trial.

•   Mr Crick has a very good lawyer and he walks free.

Explain why this ending is unusual and what moral point is being made about fairness.

....

....

....

....

....

....

Challenge

3 Here is a learner's opinion about the possible endings of *Purple Night*:

I prefer the second ending where Mr Crick walks free. It's less predictable and gives a more complicated and interesting moral message.

How do you respond to this opinion? Explain your answer in detail.

....

....

....

....

....

....

....

....

....

....

4 Time

> 4.1 Moments in time

Language focus

In fiction, writers may deliberately choose the present tense to make the events they are describing seem immediate. This can convey a character's or narrator's excitement or concern, and draw the reader in.

Look at this sentence: 'The clouds are gathering above me.' The present tense verb 'are' means the reader 'experiences' the event at the same time as the narrator. It creates tension and emphasises the drama of the moment.

Writers may also use conditional clauses and modal verbs to suggest possible *future* events or outcomes, such as in the sentences: 'The clouds are gathering above me. If the storm breaks, it will mean disaster.' Here, the conditional clause (beginning 'If') alerts the reader to the possibility of something dangerous happening in the future. The modal verb 'will' suggests the outcome. The whole sentence has the effect of hinting at a terrible outcome, creating tension as the reader waits to find out what will happen.

Focus

1   Read 'The Shadow of Flowers' by Su Tung P'o. It describes the appearance of a shadow on a paved area. Pages (servants) try to sweep it away. Annotate the poem, identifying:

- present tense verbs and a modal verb – highlight them in different colours

- the order that these verbs come in the poem – note down the effect of the placing of these verbs in the poem's structure.

The Shadow of Flowers

It piles up, thick and **formidable**,

on the **marble terrace**.

The pages, called again and again,

try to sweep it away.

But never mind, the next moon

The shadow will come back.

> **formidable:** impressive or creating fear due to large size
>
> **marble terrace:** a paved area next to a house

Practice

2 'The Shadow of Flowers' is about how natural events cannot be controlled by humans. Write a paragraph explaining how the poet's verb choices convey human feelings about nature.

....

....

....

....

....

....

....

Challenge

3 Now write your own short poem in the style of 'The Shadow of Flowers', on the same theme of human feelings about nature. Use present tense verbs and a modal verb suggesting future events. You could choose one of the following ideas, or use one of your own:

- sunrise
- sunset
- the end of summer.

....

....

....

....

....

....

....

> 4.2 Making the most of time

Carpe diem poems are about making the most of time and life. Images and figurative language such as metaphors and similes are central to the way this style of poetry is presented.

Focus

1   Read 'The Last Day of the Year' by Su Tung P'o. Annotate the poem, noting how the narrator feels about the end of the current year and the new year ahead.

> **The Last Day of the Year**
>
> The year about to end
> Is like a snake creeping into a field.
> You have no sooner seen it
> Than it has half disappeared.
> It is gone and its trouble is gone with it.
> Maybe I will have accomplished
> More next New Year's Eve.
> I should. I am still young and full of confidence.

Practice

2   The poet uses a simile that compares the passing year with *a snake creeping into a field*. Write a detailed analysis of this phrase, exploring different meanings it might suggest about the narrator's feelings.

....

....

....

....

....

....

Challenge

3   Write three different similes or metaphors to replace the snake comparison in line 2 of 'The Last Day of the Year'. Remember that most *carpe diem* poems use natural images.

a   ....

....

b   ....

....

c   ....

....

> 4.3 The tribe that time forgot

Biased writing presents a viewpoint that strongly favours one person, idea or side of an argument. Sometimes, biased texts can unfairly represent people and ideas, as they may fail to give a voice to other views.

Focus

1 Read the following article, called 'Clearing up their mess', about music festivals in England. As you read, underline words and phrases that present music festivals in a negative way

> When music festivals come to an end, all the local people are much happier. Festivals contribute nothing to the local area, apart from bringing misery for the people who live nearby. Everybody knows that at festival time, it's extremely noisy – and extremely messy. We asked some of the locals in the city of Leeds what they felt about the recent festival in their area. One resident, Karen White, said 'Festivals attract the sort of people I can't bear. They just make a mess.' Certainly today, as the festival left Leeds, there was a lot of litter lying around.

2 Analyse the overall effect of the words and phrases you underlined in Activity 2. What impression do they give the reader of people who attend music festivals?

....

....

....

....

....

....

....

Practice

3 Now think about the structure of the article. Using examples, summarise the
effect of the following structural features:

  • the regular use of broad, generalised statements about music festivals

....

....

....

....

  • the placing of Karen White's words at the end of the article

....

....

....

  • the lack of comments from anyone with a different viewpoint, such as
festival-goers, organisers or other Leeds residents.

....

....

....

....

Challenge

4 In your notebook, try writing a biased article (around 150 words) about a situation. Plan where in the structure of the piece you will use generalised statements and comments from people.

Choose one of these ideas or use one of your own:

- why soccer is really boring – an article for young people who do not like sport

- why school was brilliant – an article for older people who happily remember their school days.

> 4.4 The time tornado

> **Language focus**
>
> Verbs are usually used to show action, but they are also effective when describing events and characters. Careful verb choices can convey important shades of meaning. For example, verbs such as 'looked' or 'walked' suggest a fairly calm state of being. However, more dramatic verbs, such as 'hurled' or 'yelled', not only show action, but also suggest something about the personality and emotion of the character or scene.
>
> Writers may change the verbs they choose to create certain effects. Look at this example:
>
> - It was so strange. One moment, we were <u>chatting</u> by the river as the sun <u>looked</u> down, then without warning, the sky <u>darkened</u>, the rain <u>spat</u>, and the river violently <u>lashed</u> at the people in the rowing boat.
>
> Notice how the verbs 'chatting' and 'looked' give an impression of peace and very little movement. This is contrasted with the colour and anger suggested by 'darkened', 'spat' and 'lashed', which create a more threatening effect. The shift between quality of verbs gives a sudden sense of drama and suggests the theme of the piece – that events can change unexpectedly.

Focus

1 Look at the selection of verbs in the box on the next page.

    a Using two different colours, highlight the verbs in the box that suggest:

      • a calm mood   • a dramatic mood.

    b Annotate the verbs to show their connotations.

leapt	hurtled	whizzed	spun
rising	racing	panicking	plunged
shot	floated	opened	smiled	touched

Practice

2   Read the following extract. Write a brief summary explaining how the verb choices show a shift in mood and movement, and how they support the ideas in the paragraph.

> I leapt from the cliff and hurtled towards the water. Time and wind whizzed by and the empty sky spun around me. The water below was rising ever closer. My heart was racing. I did this for the thrill of it, but now I was panicking. What if these were the last moments of my life? I plunged into the water but I rapidly shot to the surface again. I lay there. My arms floated on the water and I opened my eyes. The sun touched my faced and smiled down. It was bliss.

....

....

....

....

....

....

Challenge

3 Write your own paragraph that shows a shift in mood from drama to calm. Choose verbs precisely to capture the changing pace of the scene. Use one of these suggestions, or your own idea:

- the last seconds of a race

- waiting for an exam result.

....

....

....

....

....

....

....

....

....

> 4.5 The visitor

When trying to create a sense of mystery, writers decide what information to give the reader and what to withhold. The combination of these structural decisions engages the reader and keeps them interested throughout the story.

Focus

1   Read this extract. Underline the key information you are given.

> It was midnight. His well-polished leather shoes strode quickly and quietly down the path. In his hand was a brown briefcase. It was locked. The contents of the briefcase were the reason why he strode quickly and quietly down the path. He pulled his hat further down and looked at the door ahead. It was locked. He carefully entered the passcode and the door opened. 'Right on time,' said a gruff voice from within the darkness.

2   Summarise the effect of this information – what impression do you have of the man and the situation?

....

....

....

....

....

....

Practice

3   Now think about what the writer *does not* tell you. Write a paragraph
summarising what is implied by the missing information, and what you think
might happen next.

....

....

....

....

....

....

Challenge

4   Write a paragraph in which you deliberately reveal and withhold information.
Try to create the effect of mystery. Use one of these suggestions or an idea of
your own:

  •   a woman walking through an airport

  •   a man running through a forest.

....

....

....

....

....

....

....

....

....

> 4.6 Into the future

The way you use and vary language when you speak is influenced by several things. For example, the place, time, topic and your audience can all affect the way you use language.

Focus

1 Describe the way you would speak and the kind of language you would use in each of these situations.

    a You are talking to a close friend about a film you both like.

        ....

        ....

    b You are talking to a new learner at your school. It is the learner's first day and you are showing her around the school.

        ....

        ....

    c You are talking to your headteacher about your plans for the future.

        ....

        ....

Practice

2 In the transcripts on the next page, Chen is talking about her hopes for the future. Summarise the variations in Chen's language between the two examples. Focus on the content and the formality of the word choices.

Chen (speaking to Ling)

I can't wait to get a job. I want to earn loads of cash. Maybe I'll be a singer. That'd be great. I'm going to earn more than you. Well, maybe! What you going to do?

Chen (speaking to her teacher)

I would like to have an interesting and well-paid career when I leave school, sir. One possibility might be music. I would really enjoy that.

....

....

....

....

....

....

Challenge

3 Write an analysis of the way Chen varies her speech in the two transcripts. Explain why she varies her speech.

....

....

....

....

....

5 ▶ That's entertainment

〉 5.1 Leaving Jamaica

Language focus

In a play, there is usually no narrator to describe and explain characters' thoughts. Instead, a playwright relies on words and actions to express such thoughts and feelings. One way writers indicate these is through a structural device called an aside. This is where a character expresses a thought aloud with the implication that other characters do not hear them. Look at this example:

MAHSA   Can you give the money back next week?

DARAB   Of course! (*aside*) What am I going to do? There's no way I can find the money before then!

The aside gives the audience extra information – that Darab cannot afford to repay Mahsa – and sets up possible conflict later in the play. Asides invite the audience to see things from a particular character's point of view, sharing their private concerns, which can establish a sense of sympathy between audience and character.

Asides also contribute to another feature of plays – dramatic irony. This is when the audience knows more than the characters on stage. Here, after hearing the aside, the audience knows that although Mahsa is expecting her money back next week, she is going to be disappointed. Dramatic irony can create effects such as humour or tension.

Focus

1   Read the short dialogue below, then note down the effect of Alexei's aside. What does it reveal about Alexei's feelings? How does it influence the audience's expectations of what might happen?

MR RAHMAN	Have you finished your project?
ALEXEI	Yes, sir. I have completed the project and will bring it in tomorrow. (*Aside*) I hope I can find the project. It isn't at home and it isn't in my bag.

....

....

....

....

Practice

2   Now read part of the conversation between Mr Rahman and Alexei that takes place the next morning. Explain the different effects of the two asides. What reaction might the audience have to the situation and the characters?

> ALEXEI   Good morning, Mr Rahman. *(Aside)* I hope he doesn't ask about the project. I think I've lost it.
>
> MR RAHMAN   Good morning, Alexei. Have you got your project? *(Aside)* What he doesn't know is that I found it at the back of the room yesterday. It's very good, but let's see what he has to say for himself!

....

....

....

....

....

....

Challenge

3   In your notebook, write your own short drama script featuring two characters who use asides to reveal things about themselves and the situation they are in. You should write at least 12 lines. Use one of the following ideas or choose your own:

  •   two sisters who have applied for the same job

  •   a boy who receives a birthday present from his best friend – he does not like the present.

› 5.2 Arriving in England

Contrast is an important structural device. Emphasising the differences between characters, settings or situations can clarify the meaning of a text for readers. Contrast can also be used to create a range of effects, from comedy to pity.

Focus

1   Read the descriptions of Gilbert and Hortense from *Small Island*. Annotate the contrasts and similarities between them. Add notes to explain why comic situations might occur.

Gilbert: A confident, energetic and likeable man from Jamaica. He is a little disorganised and often late. He is funny, dresses in colourful clothing and is happy to have a place to live, even if it is small and a little unclean. He speaks with a strong Jamaican–English accent.

Hortense: A confident but quiet and likeable woman from Jamaica. She is precise and punctual. She is very well dressed and has ambitions to make progress in life. She wants people to think of her as ladylike and has worked hard to lose her Jamaican accent, but forgets this when she is angry.

Practice

2 This scene takes place in the room that Gilbert has rented for Hortense and himself to live in. Summarise the contrasts between the characters in this extract, and explain how the audiences might react to the characters and situation.

HORTENSE	This place is disgusting! How you bring me here?!
GILBERT	Hush!
HORTENSE	I can believe you bring me all this way for a place like this! You tell me you have somewhere nice to live. You want me to live like this?!
GILBERT	Hush. No need to tell the whole . . .
HORTENSE	Get away from me! I can believe you bring me here. You live like an animal!
GILBERT	You should see the place I was living when I first arrived.

....

....

....

....

....

....

....

....

Challenge

3 In your notebook, write a short scene featuring the characters of Gilbert and Hortense. Try to capture their voices and use their contrasting characters to create a comic effect. Set your scene in a café. You should write at least 12 lines.

> 5.3 *The Boy Who Harnessed the Wind*

Language focus

Figurative language, such as metaphor, simile and personification, helps readers to understand objects and feelings by offering a point of comparison. However, figurative language can also add extra layers of meaning to the object being described. Consider this example:

- As Jin walked into the room, the air crackled with electricity.

On one level, this metaphor simply helps the reader understand the excitement Jin's entrance creates. However, the use of electricity as a metaphor opens up other layers of meaning:

- As well as giving energy, electricity is a powerful force that also has the potential to cause harm.

- Electricity has the power to transform, changing situations and people permanently.

- Electricity is generated by human effort – a combination of natural products being harnessed and used by people.

These different, sometimes contradictory, meanings in the metaphor create a more complex and more interesting image of Jin and give a greater depth of character.

Focus

1   Annotate the following simile, noting down possible meanings and ideas that emerge from it.

> Amina ran across the field, like a balloon being blown by the wind.

Practice

2   Write a detailed analysis of the different meanings of the metaphor in this sentence.

> He was a machine striding along the corridor towards that room.

....

....

....

....

Challenge

3 Write sentences using figurative language to describe the following situations.

a A boy is late for school. He runs quickly but knows that he will not arrive on time.

....

....

....

....

b A girl is very excited. She is packing to go on an adventure holiday.

....

....

....

....

c A teacher is returning to school after a long break. He is a little nervous.

....

....

....

....

> 5.4 K-pop

Different texts might explore similar ideas and themes, but they may do so in very different ways. Being able to compare both the content and style of texts is an important skill.

Focus

1   Read these two texts. They both feature young people who are committed to their work as musicians. Annotate the texts to show the key differences between the way the texts are structured and the language used.

Stardom

Every day I practised. Every hour, every day. I wanted to be a star. I knew I had the talent and I knew I had the commitment to succeed. So I did everything I was asked to. I worked as hard as I could. Every day I practised. Every hour, every day. It made no difference. My dreams of musical fame never happened.

Eddi X

We all 'know' Eddi X. He's the secretive, brilliant bass guitar player whose music has taken the rock world by storm. Nobody has seen a picture of him, yet he's played on some of the hottest music around. And why? Because he made himself the best. Years of practice when others couldn't be bothered. His commitment is the key to his success.

Practice

2 Summarise what each text shows about the theme of commitment and how you react to this information.

'Stardom':

....

....

....

....

....

'Eddi X':

....

....

....

....

....

Challenge

3 Write a comparison of the way the theme of commitment is shown in 'Stardom' and 'Eddi X'.

....

....

....

....

....

....

....

....

....

....

> 5.5 Animals and entertainment

Persuasive texts often feature political language. This commonly takes the form of powerful and emotive words and phrases that attempt to influence how the reader thinks about a topic.

Focus

1   Highlight any words and phrases in this extract that attempt to influence the reader.

> Imprisoned in small cages, the sad eyes of the tigers stare out at a world that has been torn away from them. They are like sad clowns, made to perform for people, hiding their depression behind their outward appearance. Watch them lie on the floor of their cells, depressed and unloved, and you'll agree that using animals in the circus is cruel. Set them free from their prisons. Set them free from their cruel prison guards.

Practice

2   Write a brief analysis of how the writer uses language to influence the reader's opinions about tigers.

....

....

....

....

....

....

Challenge

3   Write a paragraph that uses language to influence the reader's views about a situation involving power. You could choose one of these ideas or use one of your own:

•   the way in which animals are used unfairly by people

•   the way that powerful companies mistreat the environment.

....

....

....

....

....

....

....

....

› 5.6 The benefits of zoos

A discursive response is one that gives an objective account of several different views about a topic. This type of writing usually begins with an overview of the topic and a summary of the range of views that will be discussed.

Focus

1   Here are ten statements about zoos. Which ones are for and which ones are against the topic? Write each statement in the correct column of the table.

• Zoos are run by animal lovers.

• Animals should be free to enjoy their lives.

• Putting animals in cages is cruel.

• The love between zookeepers and animals is very strong.

• A zoo is not a natural place for an animal.

• Zoos help animals to stay alive.

• In a zoo, animals are well fed and cared for.

• Zoos only exist to make money.

• When animals live in zoos, they become weak.

• Zoos allow humans to learn about animals.

For	Against

Practice

2 Look again at the two lists. Rank the points from each list in order from 1 to 5, where the strongest point is 1.

Challenge

3 People disagree about whether it is acceptable to keep pets. What arguments might be made for and against keeping pets? In your notebook, make some notes, then write an introduction to a discursive response on the topic of keeping animals as pets. You should write at least 12 lines.

6 ▶ A sense of place

› 6.1 The city sings

Writers combine features of language and structure to build a deliberate, dramatic effect. Sometimes, writers combine language choices with other features to strengthen the point they are making.

Focus

1   Read the following extract from *If Nobody Speaks of Remarkable Things*. Underline the aural images in the text.

> The low soothing hum of air-conditioners, fanning out the heat and the smells of shops and cafes and offices across the city, winding up and winding down, long breaths layered upon each other, a lullaby hum for tired streets.

2 Summarise the overall effect created by the combination of these features.

....

....

....

Practice

3 Now think more about the combination of features within certain phrases. Summarise the effect of the following combinations.

a The long *oo* sound of a two-syllable word between two single-syllable words seen in *low soothing hum*.

....

....

....

b The use of words beginning with 'l' and the pattern of a two-syllable word following two single-syllable words in *long breaths layered*.

....

....

....

Challenge

4 Write three short phrases that use distinctive sounds or repeated letters with combinations of long and short words. Your description should focus on the sounds of the city and try to create the effect of either peacefulness or threat.

....

....

....

> 6.2 A love letter to the Grand Canyon

Romantic literature explores humans' relationship with nature. In many Romantic texts, nature is presented as a force that makes people feel a mixture of wonder and fear – a feeling known as 'the sublime'. The poem extracts below were written by the Romantic poets William Wordsworth and Samuel Taylor Coleridge.

Focus

1   Read the following lines from Wordsworth's poem 'The Prelude'. In it, the narrator describes looking up at a peak (a cliff) from his boat.

Annotate the key words that reveal the narrator's feelings about nature. What is the narrator's overriding feeling?

> a huge peak, black and huge, reared its head.
>
> the grim shape towered up between me and the stars

Practice

2   Now read a stanza from Samuel Taylor Coleridge's poem 'The Rime of the Ancient Mariner'. Here, the narrator (a sailor) describes the landscape at the South Pole, which he sees from his boat.

Summarise the scenery and the feelings it generates in the narrator.

> And now there came both mist and snow,
> And it grew **wondrous** cold:
> And ice, **mast-high**, came floating by,
> As green as **emerald**.

wondrous: strangely or delightfully

mast-high: as high as a ship's mast

emerald: a precious green stone

....

....

....

....

....

....

Challenge

3 Both texts present human reactions to nature. Write a brief comparison of these reactions, making reference to both poems.

....

....

....

....

....

....

....

....

> 6.3 Chasm

The focal character in a text is the character on which the reader focuses their attention. This might be the main character or the narrator in a story, but sometimes it may be a secondary character. Having a focal character helps the writer create different effects and reactions.

Focus

1   Read this extract, which is from a story about Jess and her sister, Melanie. Jess is the focal character.

Explain what information the reader is given about how Jess reacts to her birthday present.

> Jess opened the present. 'Oh, how kind! I love it,' said Jess. Her eyes looked at the necklace that Melanie had bought her. She didn't like it. Not one bit. In fact, she hated it. She supposed it was very kind of Melanie, but it just wasn't the type of thing that Jess liked.
>
> 'Why don't you put it on?' said Melanie.
>
> 'Yes, I will,' said Jess. 'I'll put it on tomorrow.'

....

....

....

....

Practice

2   Now read the same extract told from the point of view of Paul, Melanie's husband.

Write a summary of the differences between the two accounts and how the choice of focal character changes the meaning of the text.

Jess opened the present. 'Oh, how kind! I love it,' said Jess. Finally, thought Paul – the two sisters were getting along better than they had for years. Melanie had spent a long time choosing this gift, and it seemed to have paid off. Jess was delighted and now, so was Paul. At long last, the two sisters might stop arguing and he could get some peace.

'Why don't you put it on?' said Melanie.

'Yes, I will,' said Jess. 'I'll put it on tomorrow.'

....

....

....

....

....

....

....

Challenge

3 In your notebook, write two versions of the same situation or scene from a story, choosing a different focal character each time. You should write at least 12 lines. Choose one of these ideas or use one of your own:

- a doctor and patient conversation
- a family dinner.

> 6.4 In the desert

Sonnets are carefully structured poems with clear conventions. Some writers follow these 'rules' of sonnet writing strictly. However, others deliberately experiment with these conventions.

Focus

1 Write brief definitions of these terms.

a   sonnet

....

b   iambic pentameter

....

c   volta

....

d   couplet

....

Practice

2 Here are the first eight lines of a sonnet by Robert Frost. The poem is about an unusual bird seen in the middle of summer. Do not worry about working out the meaning of the poem just yet. Instead, think about the sonnet conventions the poet has used. Annotate the lines, identifying:

* the rhyme scheme
* whether iambic pentameter is used throughout.

The Oven Bird

There is a singer everyone has heard,

Loud, a mid-summer and a **mid-wood** bird,

Who makes the solid tree trunks sound again.

He says that leaves are old and that for flowers

mid-wood: found in the middle of a wood

> Mid-summer is to spring as one to ten.
>
> He says the early **petal-fall** is past
>
> When **pear and cherry bloom** went down in showers
>
> On sunny days a moment overcast.

petal-fall: the moment in the year where petals begin to fall

pear and cherry bloom: the flowers on pear and cherry trees

Challenge

3 In 'The Oven Bird', the narrator makes the point that in nature things begin to die away by the middle of the summer.

a Underline the words and phrases that suggest mid-summer is a time of change.

b Explain how the rhyme scheme and use of pentameter reinforces the idea of change.

....

....

....

....

....

> 6.5 Pastoral poetry

Language focus

A couplet is a common feature of poetry and dialogue in some plays. Couplets tend to rhyme and are usually placed at the end of a poem or scene. Couplets often – but not always – give a sense of 'completion', as if something is being summed up or concluded. They can be used for different effects in writing.

Here is the final couplet from a sonnet in which the narrator says that despite the length of her marriage, she is still loved:

- We were married very long ago,

  But you still love me and you tell me so.

The rhyme and the lack of caesura contribute to the sense of completion – the happiness of the narrator is reflected in the 'perfection' of the way the lines are written.

Now consider another example. Here, an older parent reflects on how they feel now their child has left home:

- My child is grown and I am sad they've gone

  Away, now I must face life on my own.

In this example, there is less feeling of completion – the writer forces the word 'Away' onto the next line and the rhyme of 'gone' and 'own' is not exact. This couplet feels much less 'perfect', reflecting the sad feelings of the narrator.

Focus

1   Look at this couplet from a sonnet about what it is like to be a child. Explain how the structure and content of the couplet reflect the feelings of the narrator.

> We played outside under the summer sun
> And all our days were days of endless fun.

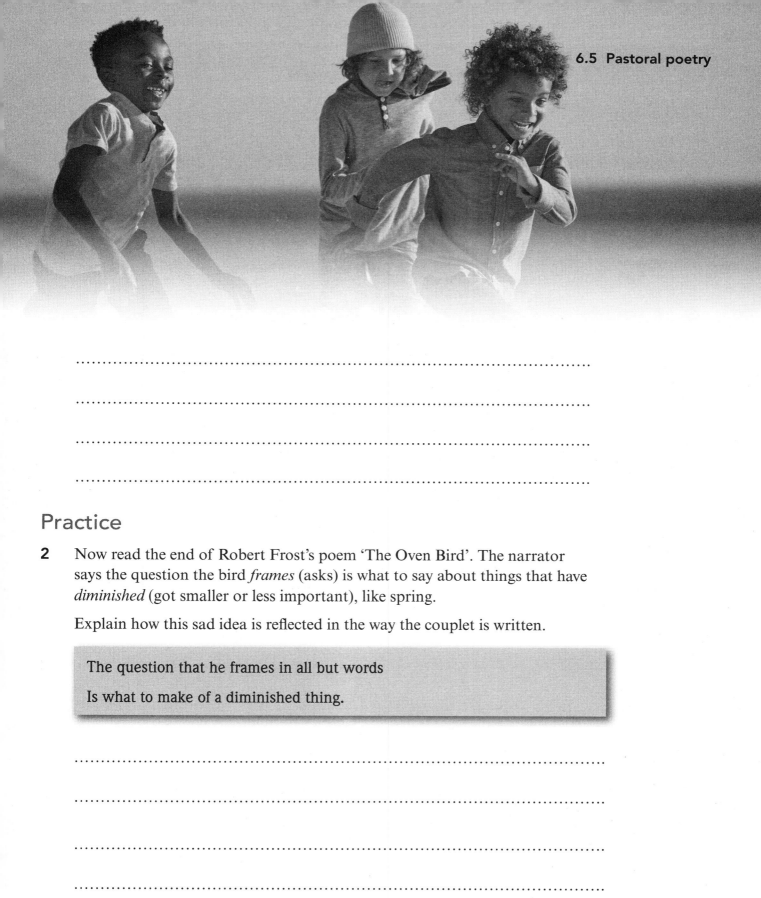

....

....

....

....

Practice

2 Now read the end of Robert Frost's poem 'The Oven Bird'. The narrator says the question the bird *frames* (asks) is what to say about things that have *diminished* (got smaller or less important), like spring.

Explain how this sad idea is reflected in the way the couplet is written.

> The question that he frames in all but words
>
> Is what to make of a diminished thing.

....

....

....

....

Challenge

3 Here is the final couplet from Shakespeare's Sonnet 19. In it, the poet is talking to a personification of Time. He says that even if Time harms his love and makes him old, the poet can still keep his love young and alive through the poems he writes.

Analyse how the way this couplet is written expresses positive and negative ideas through rhyme and caesura.

> Yet, do thy worst old Time: despite thy wrong,
>
> My love shall in my verse ever live young.

....

....

....

....

....

....

....

....

....

....

....

> 6.6 Returning home

Language focus

Pathetic fallacy is a type of figurative language where the writer uses the natural world to reflect the emotions of people in a story. For example, in pathetic fallacy, weather may embody a character's situation:

- Sidhra walked sadly along the path, her shoulders slumped. The never-ending rain soaked her to the skin.

Here, Sidhra's sadness is embodied by the rain, which is 'never-ending'. The implication is that Sidhra's sadness may also be long-lasting.

However, pathetic fallacy is more than the use of weather; it refers to anywhere that a character's emotions are projected onto an aspect of nature. Consider what is suggested here:

- Corin strode across the field, the wind blowing furiously through the long grass, whipping his legs. Up ahead was a large cliff, its rocky summit pointing aggressively to the sky.

Here, Corin's emotions are not stated explicitly in the text, they are transferred to nature. The reader understands that Corin is feeling fury and aggression.

An added effect of pathetic fallacy is that it invites the reader to anticipate what may happen later in the story. In the example, we expect some type of conflict or confrontation to occur. This creates an element of tension.

Focus

1   Annotate the following lines to show the emotions conveyed by
pathetic fallacy.

> Nafwaz walked home from the school on the last day of the year.
>
> The birds sang joyfully and the blue sky cheered.

Practice

2   Write an analysis of how pathetic fallacy is used in this extract.
Explain the emotions it conveys and the effect it is likely to have on the reader.

> Beth stormed off quickly along the narrow path. She'd never felt like
> this before. As she walked down the path, the wild winter wind yelled
> and the trees reached out their long arms to block her way. Rain clouds
> gathered angrily overhead.

....

....

....

....

....

....

....

....

Challenge

3   Write your own paragraph using pathetic fallacy to convey a character's
emotions. Choose one of the following ideas or use one of your own:

- a boy nervously walking along a dark road
- a girl arriving home after being away for a long time.

....

....

....

....

....

....

....

....

....

7 'The Journey Within'

> 7.1 The Tree

Language focus

A motif is a repeated idea or image in a text. It can be a phrase, an action or a symbol that occurs in different parts of a story. Motifs can help readers identify important themes in a text. As a motif is repeated and developed, its meanings might be extended. Look at this example of a how a wedding ring could be used a motif:

- In the first chapter of a novel, a female character gets married. Her wedding ring is a sign of love, harmony and happiness. Later in the story, it becomes a source of sadness and a symbol of memories upon the death of her husband. In the final part of the story, the woman gives the ring to her daughter for her own marriage and it comes to represent themes of renewal and family history.

Focus

1   Note down any connotations or associations with the word 'river'.

....

....

....

2   Read the extract on the next page from a novel called *The Current*. A river is used as a motif throughout the story. Summarise how the river is used to represent aspects of the narrator's life.

> When we brought baby James home for the first time, it was a beautiful morning. He was a peaceful baby, and as he slept in his cot, Francesca and I looked out of the bedroom window and wondered whether we'd make good parents. The sun lit up the meadow at the front of our house and we silently watched the small river run slowly by. It was barely moving, but we noticed the birds starting to make nests in the bank and how the small trees stood around in a conspiracy of nature. I'd never really noticed the river's gentle beauty before.

....

....

....

....

Practice

3 Now read another extract, this time from the middle of the novel. Analyse how the motif has been developed.

> Sometimes, things happen all at once. Francesca had started to feel unwell earlier that week, and within days they were operating on her. James was away at university by this time and I was on my own. As I walked through the fields that night, I didn't know what would happen. The wind raged and the river was swollen with rainwater. The water rose, threatening to burst the banks. Torrents of water tossing around sharp branches raged downstream.

....

....

....

....

Challenge

4 Write another short section of the story *The Current* that includes the motif of the river to show ideas and themes. You could describe Francesca leaving the hospital or a marriage that takes place. Write 80–100 words.

....

....

....

....

....

....

....

....

....

> 7.2 The farmers

Language focus

'Formality' refers to how serious or relaxed the language and grammar in a text are – including word choices, use of standard English, and features such as contractions, punctuation and missing verbs. In non-fiction texts, a writer will usually stick to the same level of formality throughout a text, but in fiction a writer may vary the level of formality to create specific effects. This is particularly true of dialogue, where different levels of formality can convey the status, situation and feelings of different characters. As in real life, a character's dialogue can vary in formality depending on their situation.

Continued

Look at these two examples of dialogue:

* 'I am very much afraid that I cannot allow you to proceed, sir.'
* 'You're not gettin' past me!'

The first example is very formal, with words such as *proceed* and the use of *sir* as a polite term of address. There are no contractions and the line uses standard English. The overall effect is that the speaker appears respectful, controlled and maybe even a little menacing.

The second example is much less formal. A contraction (*you're*) is used, the dropped *g* from 'getting' and the exclamation all create an impression of heightened emotion and a lack of control, or perhaps aggression.

Focus

1   The extract below is a dialogue between a mother and a daughter from a fantasy story called *Astrophile*.

Read the extract, then write a brief analysis (50 words) of the level of formality in the conversation.

'I am very proud to present to you, my precious daughter, the ring that your grandmother wore at the birth ceremony,' announced Sergot. She opened the box and the green ring sparkled in the light.

'I have no words to express my gratitude,' said Ceyla. 'It truly is the most wonderful honour to bestow upon me.'

'It is precisely as the stars decreed,' intoned Sergot.

....

....

....

....

Practice

2   Now read an extract from later in the novel. Sergot and Ceyla are running
    away from enemy forces. Read the extract, then summarise how the writer has
    used formality in the dialogue to reflect the situation.

> 'Get down!' snapped Sergot. Ceyla ducked just in time as the craft
> swooped past.
>
> 'What the . . . ?' whispered Ceyla, her voice trembling.
>
> 'They're here. Someone's told them,' said Sergot.
>
> 'But how? Why?' As Ceyla's words came out, the craft returned.
>
> 'You – that way!' And with that, Sergot vanished.

....

....

....

....

....

....

Challenge

3   In your notebook, write two conversations between the same pair of people
    in different situations. One conversation should use formal dialogue, and the
    other informal. For example, you could write one conversation between two
    brothers at a family wedding, then the second after the brothers have finished a
    tiring game of football. You should write at least 12 lines.

> 7.3 The bronze door

Fantasy fiction writers often use time as a structural device. They think carefully about the order in which to relate events, and may decide not to use a strict chronological structure. For example, they may use time shifts for dramatic effect.

Focus

1   Read a third extract from the fantasy novel *Astrophile*. What effect does the gap in time between paragraphs 1 and 2 have on the reader?

> Ceyla knew that her grandmother's ring must have some special hidden quality. There had to be a reason why it had been passed to Ceyla. Try as she might, she couldn't discover the secret, until one day, while absent-mindedly singing one of her grandmother's songs as she wandered in the garden, the green emerald on the ring began to glow. It grew bigger and the emerald opened up. Ceyla gaped in astonishment.
>
> By the time she left home later that day, everything made sense. With the secret of the ring now exposed, anything was possible. Anything at all . . .

....

....

....

....

Practice

2   Now read another extract, which takes place towards the end of the novel. Explain the effect of the flashback in paragraph 2.

> They were cornered in the ship's hold. There seemed to be no escape for Ceyla and her mother. The guards closed in. Sergot knew they would be taken to separate planets and she would never see

her daughter again. The door burst open and a group of menacing Empire guards stood in front of them. One of them laughed.

In the garden that day last summer, Ceyla had discovered that time was on her side. She had opened her mouth and sung the words of her grandmother's song, activating the ring. She'd discovered the ring was a timeshifter. All she had to do was watch the emerald open, then name a date and she would be transported to that time.

Now, trapped in the ship's hold, Ceyla remembered that moment in the garden – and she began to sing. The guard looked at her and moved closer. 'April twelfth,' said Ceyla. And then they were gone.

Suddenly, it was a spring morning. Ceyla and Sergot were standing beneath blossom trees.

....

....

....

....

....

Challenge

3 In your notebook, write a short fantasy scene that uses a gap in time or a flashback. Use language, punctuation and sentence types to suit the story and create interest for your reader.

> 7.4 The crow

A monologue is a carefully structured text. As it only features one speaker, the writer usually uses several techniques to maintain the listener's interest, including varying the plot, language and structure.

Focus

1 The text here is the opening of a monologue from a comic fantasy text. It is written from the point of view of a male character called Osric, who is lost and far from home.

Annotate the text to show how the writer has used plot, language, punctuation and sentence types to maintain the listener's interest.

> *Sound of gentle crying.*
>
> **OSRIC** Why me? I didn't ask for this quest. I am not – definitely not – the man for this job. All my life I've been told I'm not good enough. My dad told me . . . every day. (*Imitates deep masculine voice.*) 'You're a loser, Osric.' (*Back to normal voice.*) I think he meant I was not only a loser in the sense of being hopeless, but that I also lost important things. Which is not strictly accurate. For instance, this sword – the precious and only-one-of-its-kind Sword of Kyoti has never left my side since I . . . hang on, where's the sword? Is this a joke? It was here a minute ago.

Makes the reader wonder why the character is upset

Practice

2 Reread Osric's monologue. Write a short analysis of the structure, noting how the tone changes and what effect this creates.

....

....

....

....

....

....

Challenge

3   Now write the next part of Osric's monologue, using language, punctuation and sentence types to continue the story and maintain the reader's interest. (Perhaps Osric could tell the story of the Sword of Kyoti before discovering that he is sitting on it!)

....

....

....

....

....

....

....

....

> 7.5 Nothing

At a crucial point in a fiction text, the tension builds and the writer must choose whether it leads to a climax, where something very dramatic happens, or use an anti-climax to release the tension. You may think that a climax is the more exciting option, but anti-climaxes are not necessarily disappointing!

Focus

1   Analyse the effect of the anti-climax presented in this short story.

> Baz had been told not to play cricket in front of the house many times. He was a nice boy, but he also tended to forget things when it suited him. 'If I catch you once more, I'll make you stay inside for the rest of the year,' Baz's dad had warned.
>
> Baz was delighted when the bat connected with the ball and flew into the air. He'd never hit it so well. Too well, in fact, for he stood open-mouthed as the ball flew towards the window of his house, fully aware that disaster was about to occur – and incapable of preventing it. The ball seemed to move in slow motion. Baz could picture his dad's angry face growing in his mind as the ball spun ever closer to the window . . . But just as it was about to strike, his older brother's arm plucked it from the air.
>
> 'You owe me,' said Micky.

....

....

....

....

Practice

2   What would be the effect if the last two sentences were replaced with the following?

> The ball broke the window with an earth-shattering crash. A cold silence ensued, followed by his dad's voice bellowing from inside the house.

....

....

....

Challenge

3   In your notebook, write two versions of a brief story like the one in Activity 1. One should end with an anti-climax and the other with a climax. You could write about somebody waiting for an important letter or use an idea of your own. You should write at least 12 lines.

> 7.6 Chosen One

A *Bildungsroman* is a story that focuses on the development of a young person. These narratives show the main character facing different problems, which teach them important life lessons and help them to grow up.

Focus

1   Here are the opening and closing paragraphs of a fantasy novel. Write a brief summary of how these sections suggest the hero Rostin's personal growth. Use quotations from the text to support your points.

Opening paragraph

Rostin gazed from his window onto the farmyard below. His father was moving the horses and giving the men their jobs for the day. Rostin yawned and buried his nose in his phone. It had a new game on it. But soon enough, he was asleep again. He had the same dream as yesterday. In it, he was a little boy sitting behind a glass screen watching older boys run and play. They would change suddenly into men – confident, laughing and powerful. In the dream, Rostin was forever a little boy sitting watching and gradually shrinking.

Closing paragraph

It was some years later when he arrived home. The old farmyard looked the same, but his father was shuffling now as he moved the horses and tried to raise his voice to attract the men's attention. Rostin turned to his father. 'I'll do this. You go and have some breakfast indoors.' Rostin clapped his hands loudly. 'Right, men. Listen up.' The men turned to face Rostin – his confident stare and broad shoulders gave him an immediate air of authority. His voice rang around the farmyard. Inside the farmhouse, his old father smiled.

....

....

....

....

....

....

Practice

2   *Bildungsroman* texts are about personal growth, but they also explore related themes. Write an analysis of the story, explaining what it shows about the theme of father-and-son relationships.

....

....

....

....

....

....

Challenge

3 Write your own opening and closing paragraphs of a *Bildungsroman* text. You could focus on a mother-and-daughter relationship. Or you could write about a different type of relationship, such as a brother and sister who have an argument, or a teacher and a student.

Opening paragraph:

....

....

....

....

....

Closing paragraph:

....

....

....

....

....

8 ▶ Different lives

> 8.1 The aeroplane

Language focus

Conflict is the driving force in stories – every narrative needs a problem or situation for the main character to overcome. Conflicts are expressed in the overall plot, but they can also be conveyed in language choices.

Consider the words and images in these stage directions from a play about mining. Notice how the image of the cramped mine, shown in words such as 'dark' and 'enclosed', is contrasted with a sense of freedom reflected in words such as 'wide, green lawn'.

- The set allows the audience to see the dark, enclosed underground world of the miners and also the large house of the mine owner, with its wide, green lawn and apple trees.

Now look at how conflict can be shown through dialogue. Here, the words 'I need' are set against the harsh negativity of 'No!'. The symbol of chains and the idea of being bound are used to emphasis the conflict.

ARJAN	I need to be free. I need to leave home and break these chains.
DANIELA	No! Your place is here. You are bound to this family for life.

Focus

1 Summarise how language is used to present conflict in this dialogue. The two characters are 40-year-old brothers.

HELMUT	Why is it that you ignore everything I say? You must listen to me.
GUNTHER	I've spent my life listening to you. It's suffocating! I need space.
HELMUT	Nonsense! You depend on me. You always have.
GUNTHER	Not any more. Time for us to go our separate ways.

....

....

....

....

....

Practice

2   The following are some stage directions from a play called *House on the Hill,*
set in Malawi. Analyse how the writer implies conflict through the language
used in these stage directions.

> *As the stage lights come up, the audience sees a small wooden hut on
> the left of the stage. Its walls are beginning to rot and the roof doesn't
> look fully secure. A young child and his mother leave the hut. The boy's
> body is very thin and his clothes are ragged. The mother looks tired. She
> glares angrily across the stage, and the lights come up on the outside
> of a large house. From inside, laughter is heard and also the sound of
> plates and glasses. A man's face appears at the window. He is well fed
> and well dressed. He glares across the stage and closes the curtains.*

....

....

....

....

....

Challenge

3 Write your own dialogue or stage directions to suggest conflict. Make sure you choose language carefully to suggest the conflict taking place.

....

....

....

....

....

....

....

> 8.2 Mrs Manzi

Writers may choose to explore themes and ideas through contrasting characters. By structuring a story around two characters with different attitudes, the audience can see a range of perspectives about the theme being presented.

Focus

1 Read these character descriptions.

Leila is 35 and runs her own large clothing business. It employs many local people, who are paid very little for the work they do. Leila lives in a beautiful house by the river.

Jen, Leila's twin sister, has spent 15 years travelling the world working as a doctor in poor communities. She is visiting Leila for a week.

a   Summarise their contrasting features.

    ....

    ....

    ....

    ....

b   Suggest what ideas and themes could be explored through these characters.

    ....

    ....

    ....

    ....

Practice

2   Read the following extract featuring Leila and Jen.

LEILA	It's good to have you here. I've missed you. I'm glad we're speaking again.
JEN	Me too. So much has happened in fifteen years, Leila. I can't believe the size of this house. It's absolutely huge.
LEILA	You know me. I always wanted a big house – ever since I was a little girl. That and a nice car.
JEN	Yes. You must be proud.
LEILA	(slightly irritated) What do you mean?
JEN	I mean you must be proud – of all of this.

JEN *gestures to suggest the size of the house.*

LEILA	(defensively) I am. I'm successful. I make no apology for it.
JEN	Do you feel you should apologise?
LEILA	Who to? You?

JEN	Maybe the people in your factory who work for nothing. Or the people around the world who starve while rich people live in palaces.

a How is the theme of ambition explored through these contrasting characters?

....

....

....

b How do these contrasts lead to conflict?

....

....

....

....

Challenge

3 In your notebook, write a scene involving two contrasting characters. You could base it on two brothers with different skills or choose an idea of your own. You should write at least 12 lines.

> 8.3 A different voice

Both fiction and non-fiction can be told from different points of view – for example, autobiographical accounts offer different perspectives to biographical ones. The details and attitudes of the writer may vary considerably depending on who is giving the account.

Focus

The text on the next page is from an autobiographical account called 'Moving On'. It is written by Will, an 18-year-old who had a car accident that left him in a wheelchair.

I don't remember much about the accident, but when I woke up in hospital it took me a while to come to terms with things. Fortunately, my family were great. They were there every fin of the way. With their help, I realised that there were many good things in life that I could still enjoy – I was lucky in so many ways, because I was loved and cared for. One of the things that gave me joy in the early days was joining a local wheelchair basketball team. I'd played basketball at school, but it was a challenge getting the strength in my arms. I met some new and hopefully lifelong friends through the sport. I hope I can continue to play for the rest of my life.

1   Explain how Will presents his experiences. What does he state, explicitly and implicitly, about what happened to him and about the people around him?

....

....

....

....

Practice

2   Now read an account by Sarah, Will's older sister. Summarise how she presents her brother, using examples from the text.

Will is a fighter, but when he woke up in hospital after the accident, he was desperately unhappy. I was worried for a while, but I knew he'd find a way. He always does. I remember the first basketball game he played, which we attended as a family. He'd been training for months and it was a league game. Will was always modest about his skills, so we were quite shocked when we saw how many people were watching – I just didn't realise how big the sport was. I shed a tear when he led the team out as captain, and watched with absolute pride as he led them to victory. He looked stronger – and happier – than ever.

....

....

....

....

....

....

Challenge

3 Write a comparison of the two accounts. Explain the different ways in which Will's experiences are represented and the different effects this has on the reader.

....

....

....

....

....

....

....

....

> 8.4 He for she

Language focus

Choices of pronouns can be very effective in persuasive texts. For example, first-person singular pronouns, such as 'I', 'me' and 'my', make the speaker or writer sound direct and sincere:

• I am really saddened by what I have seen.

In this line, the speaker makes it clear that they have been personally affected, which is effective in convincing the audience that the speaker genuinely cares about the issue.

Continued

First-person plural pronouns, such as 'we', and second-person pronouns, such as 'you', can have different effects:

- We need to work together to change things.

- We want you to help.

In the first example, 'we' includes the audience, making it seem as if the speaker and audience are on the same side. In the second example, 'we' makes it seem as if the speaker is part of a powerful group. The 'you' in that example directly addresses the audience, inviting them to consider their responses.

Focus

1   This extract is from a speech by a teacher to their class about the challenges of exams. Write a brief explanation the effect of the pronoun choices 'I' and 'you'.

> At the end of the year, you will face the challenge of exams. I can assure you that if you work hard and listen carefully to everything I say, then you will succeed. I can promise you that I will help you as much as I can, but you also need to make a promise to yourself – that you *will* work hard. To fulfil your potential, you need to take responsibility for your own learning.

....

....

....

....

Practice

2   Here is a similar speech. Read it, then write a summary of the effects created by the variety of pronoun choices.

> At the end of the year, we face the challenge of exams. I can assure you that if we work hard and you listen carefully to everything I say, then together we will succeed. I can promise you that I will help you as much as I can, but you also need to make a promise to yourself – that you *will* work hard. The whole school is behind you – we are all in this together.

....

....

....

....

Challenge

3 Now try experimenting with different pronoun choices. Write two short speeches that use pronouns in different ways. You could write a speech from a sports team manager to the players before a big game or use an idea of your own.

Speech A:

....

....

....

....

....

Speech B:

....

....

....

....

....

....

> 8.5 The transporter

Texts that present unusual settings and experiences can provoke strong reactions from readers. Often these reactions are based on the reader's own attitudes to different genres and fiction in general.

Focus

1   Read the opening of a science-fiction story called *Bismutta*. Note down your initial reactions to the content and the use of language and structure.

> 6 September. The ship left for Bismutta. I was on board. With the *amandene*. When we got to Bismutta, the Yorg would surely search me for the *amandene*. Under no circumstances could I let them have it.
>
> 7 September. The *amandene* is gone. Power is no longer ours. The Yorg are in control. Maybe for ever. Maybe not. Much would depend on the arrival of Smith.

....

....

....

....

Practice

2   Here are two reactions to *Bismutta*. Beneath each one, summarise the response and identify any factors that have influenced the reader.

I've never been a fan of science-fiction. There's just too many odd references to unreal places and objects. By the end of the second paragraph of *Bismutta*, I didn't want to read any more. I was unsure what was happening. The style didn't help either – it was like a diary entry written in a hurry and didn't really feel like a proper book.

....

....

....

....

I enjoyed *Bismutta*. To me, fiction should be about unusual things – things you could never witness in real life. That's what I enjoyed about the book – its escapism. I had so many questions by the end of the second paragraph, such as who the narrator was, why they were travelling, what *amandene* and the Yorg were. I wanted to read on to find out the answers.

....

....

....

....

Challenge

3 Think of a book you have had a strong reaction to. Write a brief explanation of your response to it and what influenced that response.

....

....

....

....

....

....

....

....

> 8.6 A strange ship

As a story develops, the writer must use a range of features to maintain the reader's interest in the narrative. The combined effect of conflict, mystery and tension can be a powerful way to move a story forwards.

Focus

1   Read this extract from *The Monophore* – a science-fiction story in which the narrator, Zeb, arrives at a hostile planet, Medes. He is in disguise.

   Annotate the text to identify elements that create conflict, mystery and tension.

> This was it. The moment where anything could happen. Anything. I left the ship, clutching the *monophore* and hoping they wouldn't search me. The *monophore* was the answer. We needed it. Walking into the arrival hall, my mouth going dry, I tried to move unhurriedly. The Medean guards watched all the passengers, some with cases, others, like me, travelling light. The *monophore* pulsed in my hand. A Medean turned towards me. 'Hey, you!' he said. And all at once, Medean tentacles were moving towards me . . . The world stopped. The face of the guard was like wax. My legs – jelly.

Practice

2   Analyse how conflict, mystery and tension are created in *The Monophore*. Refer to the way language techniques, sentence structure and punctuation contribute to these effects.

....

....

....

....

....

....

....

....

....

Challenge

3 In your notebook, write a scene that combines conflict, mystery and tension. It could be in any genre. You could write about a person leaving their house in the dead of night or an idea of your own. Choose language techniques, sentence structure and punctuation to achieve these effects. You should write at least 12 lines.

9 Strange and unusual

› 9.1 Stranger in a strange land

Language focus

An ambiguous ending is one that is open to different interpretations. When ideas or events are left unresolved or uncertain, it can create an unsettling but powerful effect on the reader. For example, look at these final two sentences of a story:

- I looked across the water, and asked her to marry me. She was silent for a moment then uttered words I never expected to hear.

Did the woman accept the proposal or not? The reader does not know – but they are left intrigued! The reader can make up their own mind.

Ambiguous endings can also be used to suggest mixed feelings. For example:

- I packed my bags and closed the door quietly. My new life was beginning and my old one was ending.

In this example, the narrator does not confirm how they feel, which may suggest an inner conflict. The ending creates a bittersweet feeling, leaving the reader with a final impression of the narrator's uncertain situation.

Focus

1   On the next page, read the last four lines of a poem called 'Always There', about a father-and-son relationship. The poem is narrated by the son, who is now grown up and has his own family. In these lines, he thinks about his father.

Annotate the text to suggest different possible interpretations of the lines.

I grew up, and you grew old.

Was I a disappointment to you, or were you proud?

You never said.

No matter how old I am, you're always there.

Practice

2 Use your annotations to write an explanation of the different ways that the language in the ending of 'Always There' could be interpreted.

....

....

....

....

....

....

Challenge

3 Write your own final paragraph to a story or poem using an ambiguous ending. You could write about a person leaving their home country, or choose an idea of your own.

....

....

....

....

....

....

....

....

....

....

> 9.2 A strange meeting

In his plays, Shakespeare uses language in very creative ways, especially in his use of figurative language to express ideas. One of the challenges when reading Shakespeare is to try and understand the words both literally and metaphorically.

Focus

1 In this quotation, Macbeth has been thinking about his ambitions. Here, he is talking to the stars – he wants them to stop shining on him.

Annotate the text to explain the meaning of this figurative use of language.

> Stars, hide your fires;
>
> Let not light see my black and deep desires

Practice

2 Lady Macbeth gives her husband some advice – she tells him to keep his ambitions a secret so no one will know what he plans to do. In your own words, explain what she means in the following quotation.

> Look like the innocent flower,
>
> But be the **serpent** under it.

serpent: a snake

....

....

....

....

Challenge

3 In *Macbeth*, figurative language often supports
the themes of the play. One of these themes is
how people hide their true personalities.

Write an analysis of this idea by exploring
the connotations of the metaphor
used in the quotations in Activity 2.

....

....

....

....

....

....

....

> 9.3 Fun with *Macbeth*

In the hundreds of years since Shakespeare wrote *Macbeth*, there have been many
different versions of the play. Some performances use the original text and some
change it to modern English. Some change the setting altogether.

Focus

1   Read this account of a 21st-century performance of *Macbeth*. It describes Macbeth's meeting with the weird sisters. Explain your reaction to the way the sisters are presented.

> Macbeth is a general in an Eastern European army. After a battle, he returns to headquarters and meets three nurses. They are dressed in nurses' uniforms, but speak in low, threatening voices. Instead of attending to their patients, they ignore them and confront Macbeth.

....

....

....

....

Practice

Here is another description of the weird sisters, this time from a modern film version.

> The film opens in the grounds of a large, old building. Three schoolgirls are walking through the grounds. They are well dressed and look like normal students, but as the camera follows them, they begin to destroy flowers and a small brick wall.

2   Compare the way the weird sisters are presented here with the description in Activity 1.

....

....

....

....

Challenge

3   Write an analysis of what these versions of the play suggest about the weird sisters and about the theme of unnatural behaviour.

....

....

....

....

....

....

....

> 9.4 An unusual job

Writers make conscious choices about how they represent characters in fiction and real people in non-fiction texts. They shape and edit their writing to portray that person in a way that suits their intentions.

Focus

1   Here is part of a feature article on 12-year-old musician Anna Jeffs, the youngest girl to attend music college. Summarise the image of her presented by the writer.

> ### Rising Star
>
> Anna Jeffs tells me she 'wasn't expecting to be going to such a brilliant music college so soon,' but it's not hard to see why she is viewed as the best young drummer in England. As she sits in front of me, you can tell she is obsessed with rhythm – her hands and feet are constantly moving, tapping out a beat. She answers my questions, but sometimes you can see her mind wandering, always thinking about her music. This level of obsession is why she is the nation's rising star.

....

....

....

....

....

....

Practice

2 Write an analysis of the way the writer uses language to present a less positive view of Anna Jeffs in this article. Make some comparisons to the extract in Activity 1.

> ### Too Much, Too Soon
>
> Anna Jeffs is described by some as the best young drummer in England. If that is true, it comes at a cost. The young woman sitting in front of me today seems tired and distracted. I assumed she would be delighted to be attending music college, but she said 'wasn't expecting' it. Child stars often pay a high price for success, and even now you can see that she struggles to focus on questions. Her work seems to be taking its toll on her concentration – and that makes me worry for her future.

....

....

....

....

....

....

....

Challenge

3   In your notebook, write two versions of a brief article about a famous person. Make one version very positive and the other less so. Check your work afterwards to ensure accurate spelling and grammar.

〉 9.5 Unusual endings

Many texts have conventional endings – that is, they end how readers expect them to. However, some writers choose unconventional endings for their stories, to surprise or shock their readers. Each type of ending appeals to different readers.

Focus

1   Read the story synopsis, then explain how you would end it in a conventional way.

> **The Missing Watch**
>
> James is 15 years old. His mother gave him a special present – a watch. One day, he returns from a run along the beach and realises to his horror that the watch is missing. He is sure that it must be somewhere on the beach. He doesn't tell his mother, but his mother senses that something is wrong. James spends the next few days searching the beach. Several friends help him. His mother arrives at the beach and sees James. He is upset.

....

....

....

....

Practice

2 Now describe a more unusual ending to the story.

....

....

....

....

3 What moral messages does each ending suggest?

Conventional ending:

....

....

....

Unusual ending:

....

....

....

Challenge

4 Choose one of the endings and write the final paragraph of the story in your notebook. Use a variety of sentences and punctuation for effect.

> 9.6 A twist in the tail

Language focus

Many words in English have more than one meaning. For example, the word 'leaves' is a verb meaning 'departs', but it is also a noun for the green growths on plants and trees. The context of a sentence usually makes it clear which meaning a writer intends, but sometimes writers play on these double meanings to create jokes or puns for comic effect. For example, this pun relies on the two meanings of the word 'struck':

• He was trying to remember what caused lightning when it suddenly struck him.

Here, one sense of 'struck' means 'to suddenly realise', and the other means 'to be hit'. Both of these meanings work in the context of the sentence and create a light humour. Scenes or even whole stories can be based on a character misunderstanding the meaning of a word. The effect is often comic but writers can also use wordplay for tragic or other effects.

Focus

1   Each of the following words has more than one meaning. Write down two sentences for each word, using a different meaning in each sentence.

   a   shoot

   i   ....

   ii   ....

   b   date

   i   ....

   ii   ....

   c   right

   i   ....

   ii   ....

Practice

2 Explain the following puns – what two-word meanings are used in each one and what effect is created?

    a   The lady in the flower shop produced a lily from one hand and rose from her seat.

        ....

        ....

        ....

    b   I was wondering why the ball was getting larger, then it hit me.

        ....

        ....

        ....

Challenge

3 Write your own sentence containing a pun. Use one of these words with a double meaning: right, type, well, light, spring, bear, flat.

    ....

    ....

> Acknowledgements

The author and publisher acknowledge the following sources of copyright material and are grateful for the permissions granted. While every effort has been made, it has not always been possible to identify the sources of all the material used, or to trace all copyright holders. If any omissions are brought to our notice, we will be happy to include the appropriate acknowledgements on reprinting.

Unit 4: 'The Shadow of Flowers' from the original by Tu Fu, and 'The Last Day of the Year' from the original by Su Tung P'o, from *One Hundred Poems From The Chinese*, copyright ©1971 by Kenneth Rexroth. Reprinted by permission of New Directions Publishing Corp; **Unit 5:** abridged extract from *Small Island* (stage version) by Andrea Levy adapted by Helen Edmundson, NHB Modern Plays, 2019. Reproduced by permission of Nick Hern Books; **Unit 6:** abridged extract from *If Nobody Speaks of Remarkable Things* by Jon McGregor, Reproduced by permission of Houghton Mifflin Harcourt

Thanks to the following for permission to reproduce images:

Cover image created by Justin Rowe; *Inside* Unit 1 Comstock/GI; Photo By Joel Kraut/GI; Jeff Chandler/GI; DAJ/GI; Lisa-Blue/GI; Owngarden/GI; Unit 2 ©2019 Thomas M. Barwick INC/GI; Vincent Boisgard/GI; Peter Dazeley/GI; Dirk Hoffmann/GI; Islam Ibrahim/GI; Catherine MacBride/GI; Unit 3 Design Pics/John Short/GI; Archive Photos/GI; Fanjianhua/GI; Tim Gamble/GI; Unit 4 Benoitb/GI; Pataki Sandor/GI; Rytis Seskaitis/GI; Maskot/GI; Yuri_Arcurs/GI; Alex Potemkin/GI; Unit 5 Alina555/GI; Digital Vision/GI; Gary Brookshaw/GI; Sebastien Souchon/GI; Unit 6 Xià Qing/GI; Fotosearch/GI; Muratkoc/GI; ArtesiaWells/GI; Klaus Vedfelt/GI; Craig Leech/GI; Photo By Ahmad Kavousian/GI; Unit 7 Keystone/GI; Jake Danishevsky/GI; Fhm/GI; Lambert And Young/GI; Image Source/GI; Chatuwat Onkhamla/GI; Unit 8 James Heifner/GI; Nancy Brown/GI; Taiyou Nomachi/GI; Lorado/GI; Klaus Vedfelt/GI; PavelIvanov/GI; Matjaz Slanic/GI; Unit 9 Blue Images/GI; Kristianbell/GI; Rizwan Khan/GI; Maxross/GI; Artisteer/GI; Subjug/GI

Key: GI= Getty Images.